YOU can be a
to Start, R
Successful YouTube Channel

Gaming, Vlogging, Lifestyle, Beauty, Business

Find Your Brand, Work the Algorithm, Gain Subscribers & MAKE MONEY

By

Robin Berkeley

Autumn Leaf
Publishers

Design & Illustration By

Rebecca Albright

First Edition

Contents

Introduction

People dream about the lifestyles of the rich and famous all the time, from driving fast cars to dining at the finest restaurants with the most exquisite dishes the culinary arts have to offer.

While there's definitely no one-way ticket to all that jazz, one of the most effective ways to actually make a lot of money in recent years is to start a YouTube channel and build a career out of it.

Of course, things are always easier said than done, and nothing worthwhile ever really happens magically overnight. Not just anyone can be an instant YouTube sensation, no matter how easy people make it out to be. Building and maintaining a YouTube channel that actually makes money takes a lot of work and a great deal of patience, especially when you're just starting out.

But here's the thing: you don't have to go through the whole journey alone! I'm here to teach you all about the most practical, valuable, in-depth, and actionable tips and tricks and best practices on how to start a YouTube channel from scratch, whether you're already a video editing aficionado or you're starting out as a complete noob.

We'll talk about everything from picking out the best equipment and software if you're on a tight budget to how to market and actually grow and expand your reach once your channel is up and running. I can't promise that it'll be a journey without its own ups and downs, but I can promise that the trip will be so incredibly worth it.

So, strap in, gear up, and let's get started!

Qualities of a Successful YouTube Channel

With over a billion hours of videos being watched every single day, YouTube is one of the biggest powerhouses of content in the Wonderful World of the World Wide Web, and for a good reason. From random cat videos that keep your eyes glued to the screen from hours on end to serious, hard-hitting journalism about the ins and outs of politics across the globe, YouTube offers a wealth of video content for all kinds of viewers no matter what you fancy. It's basically a one-stop solution for, well, practically anything, and it only makes sense for you to want to monetize this extremely powerful tool.

While it all may seem overwhelming, fret not - the good news is that you don't have to go through this journey alone. Itching to share your fabulous fashion sense with the rest of the world, or clamoring for a piece of that cash-grab pie with your highly engaging live gaming feeds? There's nothing wrong with dreaming big, but before you even get started on embarking on this epic quest, forget the nitty-gritty for a second and let's talk about what makes you, you!

YouTube sensations don't happen overnight, and not everyone is cut out to be the Next Big Thing. But here's the secret: successful YouTube channels actually have a handful of things in common, so let's get right to it:

Content That's Hard to Resist

With the myriad of things demanding the attention of viewers on the Internet left and right, how can you make your own content stand out from the crowd? The most important thing you have to consider is to make sure that your content is really, really good. You have to be able to provide value to your viewers in order to grow your subscriber list. Your content not only has to be powerful and irresistible; it also has to be creative, relatable, engaging, and authentic. If you're watching a video and you find yourself saying, "I wish I did that" or "Why didn't I think of that?" then that's a sign of good content. Try to incorporate it into your videos, but DON'T COPY.

Never underestimate your viewers' intelligence - they'll spot a fake from a mile away. This is exactly why you should make sure you actually know what you're saying, and that you're not just regurgitating what other people are saying. Why should they listen to you? Why should they pick your channel over others'? You have to make sure that they finish every video with a sense of satisfaction and that your content is worthy of their time.

Religiously Uploaded Content (Perseverance is Key!)

You need to put in the commitment to upload videos regularly. Maintaining a YouTube channel takes a great deal of dedication; it's definitely not a cushy job where you can slack off. Creating content might look easy, but it's not! It needs your time and effort, especially if you are planning to do this by yourself (and you really can, so don't sweat it!).

You need to be able to think of great ideas, shoot them (as many times, again and again, to get your point across), edit, and do voice-overs. I'll be honest—be prepared to put in years of hard work without seeing any returns at first. If you're lucky, it can take a shorter time before you can rake in the cash. YouTube success is not an overnight thing for most people.

Figure out how fast you can produce one video and come up with a timetable that works for you so you can upload content for your viewers regularly without putting too much stress on yourself. Doing so helps in creating a regular following, and since we all know that a human's attention span gets shorter and shorter as time goes by, uploading regularly reminds your viewers that you are still active and creating the content that they are looking for. Also, keep in mind that quality is always better than quantity—no use pushing out halfhearted content every day if it's no good.

A lot of YouTubers start off doing it part-time, and depending on the traction they get, they might end up doing it full time. With all this, you need to remember to have fun and enjoy yourself. In the end, it's your passion for this that will keep you going.

An Ideal Niche Market

This move might seem like you're limiting your audience share, but this will actually make you stand out. You will be a newcomer in an already bustling and all-too-crowded world and will be competing against established brands who've been in the game for much longer than you have. It will definitely be a huge plus if you can find a niche that you can wedge your channel into. Find something unique - something you feel that only you can do. Add a twist or a flair that will make you shine. It might be your unique personality or a different way of showing things.

Love fashion? Look up and watch fashion YouTubers and research them and their style. Find something that they haven't done before and work on that. In the end, you will be marketing your YouTube channel yourself, and finding a niche market can help you cement a solid following.

Once you've already figured out where your channel stands, you will need to be able to stick to it. Ask yourself: will you be able to expound on this market share you've picked? Will you be able to produce content after content under this niche? Also, since you're just starting out, it will be helpful if you don't deviate, because you need to build a proper following first. Only then can you think about expanding after that. Remember: people are looking for specific content that attracts them, and you want to make sure that the content that keeps them in place is yours.

Good Social Media Management

In this increasingly mobile world, a person's social media presence is like a ghostly third arm. It's invariably connected to you, and the same goes for your YouTube channel. This is why you need to promote your content consistently across all platforms and make sure all of them are linked back to your channel—it's a great way to put yourself out there as a YouTube creator. Maintaining a well-managed social media presence can really help you rake in those views, which may, in turn, boost your subscriber numbers. One of those coveted social media shares might just be the thing that could make one of your videos go viral—you just never know, right?

Posting updates on your social media accounts can keep your channel fresh in the minds of your existing subscribers, while releasing quick, catchy snippets of your videos on Instagram, Facebook, and Twitter is a great way to attract viewers new and old. You can also release teasers that could function as ads. Think of your channel as a brand. How will you market it? Do you start with a gimmick? Giveaways? How can you let your future viewers know that you exist and you are what they are looking for? How can you reel them in to watch your content and keep them there? Knowing what to post, when to post, and what to say has a huge effect. Remember: utilizing and managing your social media accounts well goes hand-in-hand with creating quality content for your channel, as these accounts will be an indispensable tool for promoting your channel.

Interaction with Your Viewers and Other YouTubers Alike

One of the awesome things about being a YouTube creator is having your own fanbase. As it is, your goal is to have a community of subscribers who would be loyal to your channel because they would be more inclined to watch, like, and share your videos. To do this, you need to work on getting more viewers to subscribe to your channel. Let's not forget that it will also help a lot if you have a relatable brand image or a friendly and engaging online persona. Remember: human interaction is important! You definitely wouldn't want people to feel like they're talking to a manufactured drone.

So, to get more subscribers, YouTubers tend to think of creative ways on how to reel the viewers in—and one of the key points is interaction.

Here's the deal: simply interacting with your viewers is one thing—we'll talk about that later. But interacting or collaborating with other YouTubers in the same field or not (if you can think of an angle) can also be a platform to boost your channel. Think about it this way: let's say YouTuber A has a million subscribers. Collaborating with YouTuber A means her million subscribers can also see your videos, and some of them, after watching your content, might subscribe to you too! Collaboration can mean a handful of different things, but in the end, it's basically a give-and-take situation. What would the other party get out of collaborating with you? It might be easier to approach a YouTuber with around the same number of subscribers as you do and plan a collab. You could come up with a 2-part video split between both your channels. This way, viewers would have to click on both your videos to get the whole story. You could also consider showing up on their channel for a one-off project. A simple shoutout can work wonders too!

Now, I'm not saying you can't do a collab with a more popular YouTuber. You just need to come up with an angle or offer them something that you feel only you can give. Lay it all out on the table. Be confident and show them your passion for this. In the end, they are looking for that human connection—people tend to work with people they're comfortable with. Be yourself, but also be creative and try to think out of the box!

As for your interactions with subscribers, you'll have different ways on how to go about it. The main thing is to make them feel like they are part of your community or family. If you do this right, interacting with your viewers will make them feel that you're more approachable and relatable. It could be as simple as giving shoutouts or replying and liking to the first few comments that catch your eye. You could also give them options or ask for their opinions on how or what they want to see on your channel. And if you have a budget, giveaways can be good too! Make them feel that they are a part of your channel, as it should because it's their support that will keep your channel going. Lastly, always remember to treat them with love and respect, because if you plan on doing this as your full-time job, both will go a long way.

How to Set Up a YouTube Channel

So, if you've figured that you already have the right qualities, then let's delve right in on how to start your own YouTube channel in detail.

What Your Channel Will Be All About

We already talked about this before, and you might already have a clear view of what you want to talk about in your channel, or maybe you have tons of topics inside your head, all competing against each other. This is perfectly understandable. Here are two things that can help you— research and experiments.

Now, this might sound boring but hear me out. This will help you narrow it down and save you from the future pain of trial and error—not to say that you won't be doing that in the future, but this will definitely lessen it and save you a great deal of time and effort. That aside, It will help a lot if you list out all the topics in your brain and do your research about every single one of them. To help you out with this, you can use Google Trends to figure out how your topics will fare (it's free!). It will show how many times your chosen topic was searched for on the internet, therefore showing how popular it is.

When in doubt, keep this in mind: all topics are interesting, however obscure they might be. Are you vlogging about how to make glass bubbles? Do you do tutorials on woodworking and other household handicrafts? Or are you just talking about random things like observing the microscopic ecosystem that grows over a week inside a jar with swamp water in it (this is actually a real thing—I kid you not)?

Whatever your topic might be, someone out there will still watch them. The important thing is to be consistent. If you're leaning a little bit toward the apprehensive side, you can always look for a topic that is on the upward trend, or at least something stable. Keep in mind that trends will come and go. What's popular this year might not be popular in the next year, so try to think of something that will sustain the interest of your audiences for a long, long time.

You could also try various keyword search engines, but they will usually ask you to pay for their services. So, if you have the extra budget, you can use them; if not, you can always try the other approach—which is searching for your topic on YouTube itself. You will be hitting two birds with one stone with this one as you can see how popular your topic will be and how it would fare by looking at the number of views from existing videos. At the same time, doing this will also help you check out the competition—yes, my dears, competitor research.

Since you will be thinking of doing this to earn money in the long run, or to be famous (we can all be honest here), this is, ultimately, marketing yourself. You need to look for your "competitors." These are the people who are also doing videos under the same topic you're planning to do. Study them well, and look at how they are presenting their ideas, their styles, transitions, and so on. List down the videos that are raking in those views. By doing this, you can have an idea of what works well.

Here's another tip: you can write down all the ideas for a video you can come up with under your chosen topic. The more, the better! It's usually a bad sign if you're struggling to come up with a ton of ideas early on because you need to be able to constantly churn out ideas to keep your channel going. Remember what I said earlier: regular uploads.

If by some unfortunate twist of fate, you find it extremely difficult to come up with a bunch of topics for your planned channel, it doesn't mean that you need to give up on it altogether. You can always try to look at things from a different angle. What exactly do I mean by that?

Say you're thinking about doing a topic on Photoshop tutorials. You roll your shoulders, flex your fingers, and—with a glint in your eye and an unstoppable go-getter attitude—you boot up your computer and check out all the videos on the topic on YouTube. To your complete and utter dismay, you find that there are already heaps and heaps of tutorials on Photoshop existing out there—how can you possibly make yourself stand out?

Before you rage-quit and flip tables and call it a day, think about a different angle. Is it possible to narrow down such a broad topic? What kind of Photoshop tutorials can you do? Is there anything new that you can offer viewers that the others haven't offered them before? What else can you bring to the table?

Here's an example: you can try to do tutorials that focus solely on removing the background from an image. You can narrow this down further by teaching people how to use a plain white background instead. Focus on this more by targeting small business owners who want to open their own online shop—how can they make the images of the products they're selling as clean and clear as can be? How can they retouch product photos in the best way possible to boost their sales? This alone can already help you grab a huge chunk of the YouTube market, so to speak. You can even inject a little bit of humor in there if you want to—funny stuff is always a hit!

You're only starting out, after all, so let's be honest: you won't have a lot of subscribers right away from the get-go unless you're already some kind of celebrity. But if you already have a channel lying around, you can try posting videos of your chosen topics to get the feel of it. The more you post, the more you'll learn. It may be a huge cliche, but experience is always the best teacher!

Create Your YouTube channel

Now that you have figured out your topic, congratulations! Next comes creating an account. Since YouTube is owned by Google, you will need to have a Google account on hand. Using that Google Account, you can now sign in on YouTube and create your channel. You have two choices: create a personal channel where only you can manage your account or a channel with a business or another name. Most YouTubers looking to earn money would pick the latter.

For the personal channel, it's fairly straightforward. Log in to your YouTube account—desktop or mobile; it doesn't matter—then try anything that you would do with a channel, like uploading videos, commenting, or creating a playlist. If you don't have a channel, a prompt will ask you to create one. Enter your details and confirm. Viola! You have a channel! Most people will have this personal channel already if you regularly use YouTube. If you have a playlist and can post comments, then you should already have a personal one.

Next, for the business channel—again, most YouTubers will use this—this can have multiple people managing it, which can be useful in the future when your channel has grown big enough to necessitate hiring a team to work for you (still, some people do this so they can just concentrate on creating content). For this, you can use your Google Brand Account, or you can just create a new channel. Using your desktop or laptop (it's easier), go to your channel list, which can be found under "Settings" on your YouTube account. Click "Add or manage account," then select "Create a new channel." This will direct you to create a Brand Account. Fill out the Brand Account name, click "Create" and you now have your own channel. Yay!

Customizing Your Channel

When you click "Your Channel," which is located on the drop-down drawer when you click your profile pic on the upper right-hand side of YouTube, you'll be brought to a page with two blue buttons on the upper right-hand side of the screen that says, "Customize Channel" and "YouTube Studio." In "Customize Channel," under "About," you can add your channel description. You can add keywords here to improve your chances to be discovered by viewers when they search for videos. You can also add links to your other social media platforms or to your website (limit of 5 links). This will appear overlaid on your channel art.

By clicking "Add channel art" (this is the blue button in the middle of the banner up top), you can change your channel art. If the blue button is not there, click the pen icon on the upper right corner, then click "Edit channel art." The channel art appears as a banner on top of your page when people visit your channel. Change your profile pic here, too, by clicking the pen icon on the upper left-hand side of the banner.

If you are using a Brand Account, when you click "Change," you'll be notified that your profile pic comes from your Google Account (since it is connected). If you click "Edit," you'll be brought to your "About Me" page in Google. Clicking the pen icon on the right of your default profile pic will allow you to change it across your Google Account. We'll talk more about these later when we're talking about branding your channel.

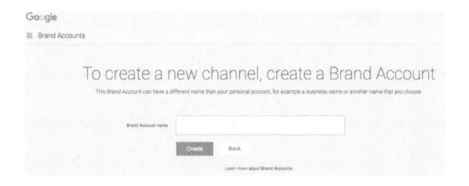

You'll also see a gear icon on the upper right-hand side of your screen. Clicking this gear will bring up your channel settings. Under "Customize the layout of your channel," click "Advanced settings" and you'll be able to set your country and enter keywords about your channel. Type in everything you can think of that could describe your channel. What is it about? Will it be about you? Vlog? Reporting? Trivia? Pets?

Food? Hobbies? Under what topic? Like you did in the channel description, these keywords will help people discover your channel. The more detailed it is, the better your chances of showing up on YouTube searches will be, which can mean more potential viewers! Think of this like the hashtags you put on Instagram but without the hash key.

Also, on this page, you can link your AdWords account and your Google Analytics property tracking ID. After making the necessary changes that you deem fit, click "Save," and from here, you can access YouTube Studio by clicking "Return to YouTube Studio."

Channel settings

Privacy

Keep all my liked videos and saved playlists private

Keep all my subscriptions private

Access more options in Account settings.

Customize the layout of your channel

Recommended for people who upload videos regularly. Add a channel trailer, suggest content for your subscribers, and organize all your videos and playlists into sections.

Access more options in Advanced settings.

Show discussion tab

Allow your fans to comment on your channel.

Translate info

Reach audiences in foreign countries by translating channel info.

Cancel   Save

It is inside this YouTube Studio where you can handle all your creator stuff. This will be your main control room as a creator, as you can do almost everything from here. Your videos are here, your comments are here, and your analytics are also here. You can also put in subtitles for your videos on this page (international audience, yay!).

Most importantly, you can also go to monetization from here. Everything and anything can be accessed on the toolbar on your left, which is under your profile pic. Another gear icon at the bottom of this toolbar allows you to access "Settings." You can further customize your channel here. Explore! Tweak! Not every channel is similar.

Up next is verifying your channel. Verifying your channel is actually easy—you just need to click your channel icon, click "Settings," then click "Channel status and features." Click the blue button beside your icon that says "Verify." I suggest that you have your mobile phone within reach during this stage because after you have entered your country, you will receive a call or a text from YouTube, whichever you picked from the options.

Enter the code you receive and click "Submit." When you go back, you'll see that your account is now verified. Now that you have your channel verified, you are now allowed to post videos that are longer than 15 mins, live stream, and appeal content ID claims. You can also set custom thumbnails for your videos! This is also as important as your title because humans are visual animals and images register faster in the brain before text does. So, being able to make a custom thumbnail will be a great addition as it can help you attract viewers. Also, it will be good for your branding.

The verification badge, on the other hand, is an entirely different thing. This is when you see a checkmark next to the channel's name. You can submit a request for this when you have finally reached 100k subscribers. And finally, after all that clicking and tweaking, you have just finished setting up your own YouTube channel. Hooray!

How to Brand Your Channel

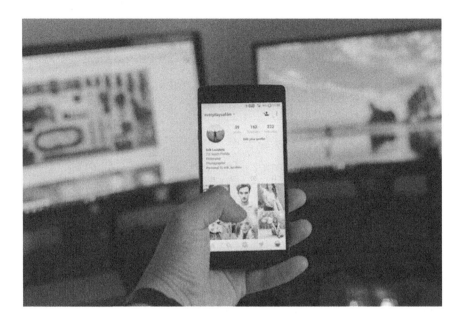

If you take the time to observe the more popular YouTubers, you'll notice one thing: everything has this same look going on, from the logo to the video thumbnails. This makes everything look cohesive, clean, and easy to understand. You'll find that you are able to identify the YouTuber by just looking at their video thumbnail. This is the recall you are going for. I'm going to walk you through just that so you'll have a style or branding that people will associate your channel with, which, in turn, will make you more memorable.

Think about it: when somebody mentions McDonald's, what image comes to mind immediately? You may think about the golden arches forming the letter "M" or the vibrant red and yellow colors that pop out from afar. You may think of the delectable smell of crispy fries that wafts in from the kitchen as you step through the doors into the fast-food joint. You may instantly recall fond childhood memories of sweet sundaes with the family or milkshakes with your best friends. You may think about biting into the juiciest burgers in the company of loved ones, or of the din and the laughter as you're surrounded by lively chatter and pleasant conversation.

Not all of these feelings that the mention of the brand evokes are intentional—all these may just be from your own subconscious even if you're not aware of it. That's the ultimate power of branding—it helps you build an image in your mind and in your heart about a certain product or service. Wouldn't you want your viewers to experience the same kind of epiphany whenever your channel is brought up in casual conversation?

Let us start with the basics. To build the brand identity of your channel, start with your voice. This is the image you would want to project with how you present your videos. Since you already have your topic in mind, think of how you would want to present it. Are you going to be friendly? Relatable? Informative? A serious journalist? Quirky? A moody hipster? This should definitely be in line with your own personality—remember that people can spot fakes from a mile away, so it pays to be genuine.

Next, pinpoint your target audience. What do they like? What's their age range? What are their online habits and behaviors? At the risk of looking like a creepy stalker, you have to find out their likes, dislikes, quirks, and idiosyncrasies. You should be completely obsessed with your audience—you can find all of this info from conducting market research.

Market research is a different beast altogether—even huge multinational conglomerates hire third-party marketing teams to study their markets and figure out what makes them tick. So that you can have a better picture of just how important market research is to any brand, think about the big video game company Nintendo. When video game consoles were just starting out, Nintendo was unstoppable— the corporate giant was dominating the industry with more than 90% of the market share at the time. Sega, an up-and-comer in the same industry, had all-too-many difficulties trying to keep up. While Nintendo was only operating on 8-bit with their games, Sega already had a much more technologically advanced 16-bit engine working for them—but not even a stronger physical performance in the console could help them outmatch Nintendo in any way.

To get them out of this dilemma, they came up with a strong marketing plan on how to make their mark in the industry—and this involved a solid foundation of market research. Since Nintendo was marketing their games to a younger market at the time, Sega decided to grab the untouched market share from the older bracket: the teens. To do this, they studied the behaviors, wants, and needs of teenagers. How do they behave? What's important to them? How do they want their games to play out, and what factors will keep them hooked onto their screens?

The answer came in the form of Sonic the Hedgehog—a fast, reckless, bright blue hedgehog with snazzy sneakers and a no-nonsense attitude. Sonic's personality—and his penchant for speed, speed, speed—instantly clicked with teenagers way more than Nintendo's cute plumber Mario did during that time, and this helped Sega rise to the top and be at par with

Nintendo. Of course, Nintendo is still going strong today with Sega lagging behind again, but I digress—that's a different story altogether.

The point is that knowing your target market inside and out is crucial to any branding strategy, no matter which industry you may be in.

With these in mind, it's time to start building your brand identity. You will be using your voice to reach out to your target market, playing into what they need and want. Start with your logo or icon; you can also use your photo if you're a vlogger. Extend this branding to your channel art, video thumbnails, and video watermark if you want one. To make things easier, you can try making a simple style guide, but a mood board will also do for starters. Pick a color palette or set of colors that you will use in your channel, and if you are a business, you should use your brand colors. Your fonts and graphics should also work well with your branding.

Build a Template for Your Video Thumbnails

Some people, like the vloggers or the more modern channels, go for a more organic approach. Some great examples of this style can be seen on Vox and a few vloggers like "best dressed." Vox, of course, has an art director to do those thumbnails for them (you can do it yourself too if you're good with design and layout). The result is an effectively recognizable video thumbnail anywhere. This is effective because when their videos come up in your recommended feed, you know that it's one of theirs, with those bright yellow accents and boxed headlines. They have since branched out from this style as their channel grows with different subtopics, but they still have this same set of colors and graphic style that proudly screams their brand. Some vloggers, on the other hand, have a more scrapbook-y feel, with hand-lettered fonts and quirky cutouts to boot.

Make Use of Palettes

To do this, you'll need to have a few fonts and graphics you'll have on hand that you will use to play around with. The trick here is to have a specific color palette and to adjust the color of your pictures. This is called color grading.

Take a look at some of the more famous Instagrammers. If you look at their feed, every shot has more or less the same feel: cool or warm, high saturation, or black and white. Some even go as far as choosing a predominant hue. It makes everything pleasant to look at, cohesive, and not scattered all over the place. This can be done easily with Adobe Photoshop or Lightroom. You can also use simple photo editing apps on your phone like VSCO.

Lightroom and VSCO have presets that you can use as a beginner. This same color grading trick can also be applied to the video thumbnail and your video itself. When done right and you have your own style, it can greatly help with your brand recall. Just pair it with your selected fonts and graphics, and you'll be good to go!

Consider Uniform Templates

On the other hand, some people would prefer to make their thumbnails look uniform all throughout. This is easier to pull off as you will have a set template that you can use over and over again—you'll only need to change the text and pictures every time you have a new video. This way, you won't be pressured to think of a new layout every time you have a new one coming up (again, don't forget to color grade your pictures). This works best if you are leaning more on the informative or minimalist side.

Let's say you do video editing tutorials on your channel. This style should be distinctive and informative enough that they will click on your video if they search for a topic, and your video comes out, especially if you already have the brand recall you're aiming for. Another thing to note is that your target audience, once they are in your channel, will definitely have an easier time browsing through your videos to look for the specific topic they are interested in.

Keep Thumbnails Consistent

With either approach, especially with the organic style, try to keep them consistent and looking like they belong with each other for easier recall. You will be building your brand recognition, after all—plus, you will also be making it easier for yourself when you are branching out to other subtopics in the future.

Let's say you are originally doing DIY videos, but somewhere along the way, your viewers decide they want to see more vlogs from you. With a consistent set of brand guidelines, you can just easily incorporate your original thumbnail layout and make a new one using the same elements by shifting the color or the elements around a bit.

Another way is to make a mini "flag" or "call out" to be

placed on the edge of your thumbnails. Want to position it at the bottom? On the right? Left? It's totally your choice. This is to separate them from your original content, and don't forget to utilize the playlists too! Subdivide the categories of your videos to make them easier for your viewers to browse through. You don't want your subscribers to slug through hundreds of your videos just to find that series of DIY cat mufflers you did a year ago. If it takes them forever to find it, they will quit mid-scroll.

I know this is a lot to go through just for video thumbnails, but I just can't stress this enough. The thumbnails are going to be the first thing that attracts the viewers' eyes when they're searching for videos. Well-made and eye-catching thumbnails are sure to attract viewers. Think of this as the packaging of goods in grocery stores—companies and brands invest large sums of money to have designers create good packaging. It might seem unimportant as you throw it away after opening or using it, but ultimately, it's what attracts your eyes first. It makes you want to touch the product, inspect it, and hopefully even buy it.

It's the same thing with your thumbnails—viewers scroll really quickly sometimes, and you only have a few seconds tops to attract their attention. The solution then is to make it interesting enough—or, for lack of a better term, clickbait-y enough—to make your viewers click and enjoy.

Don't Forget Your Channel Art

To recap, the channel art is the banner up top that viewers see when they visit your channel. A lot of first time YouTubers make the mistake of making this image static and never changing. Don't make the same mistake! Treat this as a billboard for your channel or your calling card. As I mentioned above, you can put links to your website or your various social media accounts here. If you are going to use YouTube as a social media extension of your business or your brand, this space will be a great place to advertise it.

You can even advertise how often you post new videos here. Use catchy phrases like "check back every Tuesday at 8 am for new barbeque videos!" or something to that effect. You can also use this space to promote your new videos, a new channel, or a new segment. I suggest changing this banner every time you have something new happening in your channel. Are you a business with a new product? Advertise it here. It's basically like a billboard that you don't have to pay for, so utilize it well.

Brand Your Content, and Yourself

Now let's talk about the branding for your videos itself. The things I've been talking about above are meant to catch your viewers attention. We can consider them as the outer layers of your content, like the gift wrap or packaging. This time, we are going to talk about the meaty, juicy inside, which means your videos or the content itself.

You might be thinking, "Does branding apply to this stuff too?" Why, yes, it does! I mean, you'd definitely want to hook passing or casual viewers with your amazing content and turn them into active subscribers, right?

We live in a consumer-driven world, and everything is out there to please or attract you and make you want or need things. Corporations invest millions and strive to turn your "want" into a "need" and to make you buy their products repeatedly. Case in point: Nike comes up with new basketball shoes that they say make you jump higher. Sneakerheads and basketball enthusiasts "need" it, which translates to a sale. See the trick?

Now, I'm not saying you should go ahead and trick your viewers. Remember when I said that they spot fakes from a mile away? Plus, they will talk about you in forums, and word spreads fast in the World Wide Web (alas, such are the woes of becoming famous).

What you actually need to do is to curate yourself. For example, if you are a lifestyle vlogger, you should try to show viewers your stylish, graceful side. This is the side that viewers would like to see and would like to emulate. Here's a different angle: you're also a lifestyle vlogger, but you show your fun and quirky side. This is the cool friend that they all want to hang out with, that person that will make them laugh, or that older sibling that viewers wish they had. You might even be someone that they feel like they can confide in. It's still you—but refined and curated.

Love Your Target Market, but Love Yourself Too

When it comes to catering to your target market, I know a lot of you are thinking, "I just want to enjoy myself and do things that I like!" Of course, not everything should be for your viewers, which is why you should try to find the perfect balance between their needs and yours. If you do everything in your power to cater to their wants and needs, what about yours? Have you forgotten about your own interests and your own views?

Once you stop thinking about yourself, your viewers will become consumers to you, and you will lose that human interaction that makes everyone love YouTube creators. This will turn into a regular job that you might soon hate. This whole thing should be something that you're passionate about but just so happens to earn you lots of cash—isn't that why you wanted to be a YouTuber in the first place?

Ask yourself, "Is this what I will find myself watching when I'm on a YouTube binge? Do I find this entertaining? Do I love this?" Create videos that you yourself would find interesting and would spend countless hours watching. When you're ultimately enjoying yourself while doing this, you won't struggle to think of new ideas. If you're enjoying yourself, it will be evident in your work, and most viewers will see that and find it engaging.

So again, find a middle ground—somewhere you would place it in the market but at the same time keep it close to your heart. It's a balancing act, really, the way you would brand your channel. It's better to start with something you love, tweak it, and curate it for your viewers. Then you can use your branding to attract viewers and keep them watching the videos that you love creating with how you talk, how you dress, how you edit your videos, your music choices, and even to your scripts.

Take the time to make your scripts

Scripts? You don't want to write scripts, you say? Not good with words? That's totally fine—you just need an outline, then make it up as you go along. Inspiration works like that sometimes. You can just edit it afterward, then reshoot and edit again. Every creative process is different—there is no same path to creativity. Not every video needs scripts, anyway. Of course, if you have a more informative type of channel, you need scripts. But if you do ASMR videos or something along those lines, you can totally get away with no scripts—you just need storyboards. Ha!

Kidding aside, all I'm trying to say is you need a plan or a direction to guide you along. I call them scripts for simplicity's sake—some people like to call it storyboarding, but it's more like an outline of what you want to do in your video. It's pretty generic: you start with a beginning, which is usually your introduction, then proceed with the middle, which is the main content. Then, you come up with the ending, and that's that. Every show you watch is following some sort of outline or script.

Look back and remember all the shows you watched before. Yep, everything has a script—just remember that once you start with one style, you shouldn't diverge from your format too much. And keep your branding in mind! Ask yourself, "Is this me? Is this my channel? Does it fit in with all the other videos?" If it doesn't, and you really want to produce it, then you'd better make another category or a sub-channel. Having an outline as you shoot your videos will also save you a lot of time shuffling about. It ultimately saves a lot of time editing too.

Editing is Your Friend

Speaking of editing, pick an editing style that fits your channel branding. If you're a thrift store fashion channel, the 90's style editing could work for you. Featuring daily life and a bunch of relaxing vlogs? A lot of still shots and slow pans and scenic montages would work beautifully. Just remember to match this with what your content is. Scenic montages won't work with documentary videos about the current political climate, of course. You will find your editing style with the more videos you edit, so keep at it, and you will get better. Just remember to start with your branding as your base, then slowly move along and improve. It's just like drawing—use the basics like anatomy as your starting point before you try experimenting with illustration styles. Develop an editing style that is unmistakably yours but also works well with your brand.

Don't Stop the Music

Background music needs to be chosen very, very carefully because music adds an extra oomph to your videos. Even silent films back then weren't really silent—they had a whole orchestra accompaniment with them. So imagine you're a lifestyle vlogger who has this graceful, French chic image...and your video montage is set to death metal. That's just too jarring!

Find music that helps with your branding and is totally you at the same time. The music should definitely be something you actually like because realistically, you'll be hearing it again and again when editing. If your target audiences are tween girls around 12 to 14 years old, then you probably don't want to use old jazz music or early 2000's emo.

Trivia: did you know that brands pay huge sums of money just to have the perfect playlist for you to shop in? They only play music that caters to their market, as it adds this certain feeling that makes you feel happy and energized when shopping. It's the same thing with the scent that you smell when you enter stores. Yes, branding attacks all senses.

That said, you can't just pop in the latest Justin Bieber or Coldplay song and use it in your video. You need to use music that's FREE or your videos will be taken down by copyright, and fast. There are sites out there that offer music that you can use on your videos: Soundcloud, Amazon Music, or Epidemic sounds, to name a few. Most of them have subscription fees, mind you, but some tracks on Soundcloud are free to use. Most of the songs that you can use from here are under Creative Commons, and as you can probably sense by now, there are various copyright laws and licensing issues involved with this.

Don't worry; I'm here to help you, right? Here's a quick guide:

First up is "Creative Commons." The main thing about "Creative Commons" is that the musician or sometimes the licensor gets the credit for the music they create. So, music that is protected under this license usually specifies what you need to do or provide in order to use their music in your videos. This means that you are free to use the songs, but you need to follow the rules set by the artist.

Then comes "Royalty-free," which a lot of people mistake as free. It's totally NOT. This only means that you pay the artist or the licensor ONLY ONCE for the music that you would use, and you can use it as many times as you can possibly want. You wouldn't need to pay the artist or licensor royalties for every time you use the song. This applies in stock photos and videos too.

And finally, "Public Domain." This music is totally FREE. If all rights to the music have already expired—it differs per country, so check carefully—then it's on "Public Domain." This means you can do anything and everything with the music under this without paying a single cent.

That said, be careful with your music choices. It's already hard to find the perfect soundtrack to your road trip with friends, so finding music that fits you, is in line with your branding, and won't have you sued is twice as hard. I suggest sticking with free sites first; you can pay for subscription services later when your channel is already up and running. There is an easier way, of course, because YouTube actually has an audio library located within your YouTube Studio.

You can even monetize your videos that have songs from the YouTube Audio library because even some tracks under "Creative Commons" still specify that you can't monetize them.

In summary, branding is everything, and if you do it right, it can help your channel a lot. Since you're building your channel from the ground up, you absolutely need brand recognition to compete with other existing and new YouTubers. And for you to build brand recognition, you need to find a style or a look that is uniquely you.

Use branding as a means to further connect with your viewers or attract them, because as they say, "People fall in love with people." So, you build your channel using your branding as your guide, but don't forget to keep it tied to your likes and preferences as you are. Think of it this way: you create videos about content that interests you for people who like the same interests. In the end, you would want viewers to go to your channel by default—or, better yet, to actively seek out your channel when they are looking for videos of your specific topic. Again, this is slightly different if you are a business—you also use branding as a way to reach your target market and to give that human feel to it. But instead of thinking about the branding and your preferences, businesses think about the branding and the brand itself.

Before You Can Make Money

How to Shoot and Pick Your Ideal Camera Equipment (Depending on Your Budget)

Now let's talk about cameras you're going to use for shooting your content. Contrary to popular belief that you need super expensive video equipment to start your own YouTube channel, you can actually start by just using your phone. Yes, that's right, your phone. New phone cameras can actually rival some DSLR cameras, especially if you know what you're doing.

Your phone cameras have come a long way from that pixelated mess that you had in your hands in the early 2000s. Phone manufacturers now are actually competing with their camera specs. I mean, they shot a movie in Taiwan using just an iPhone X Max, and it had already won 3 awards in international film festivals. They shot an award-winning movie with a 2018 iPhone, so who says you can't shoot your YouTube videos with one?

Still, it helps to actually know what you're doing—that's the basic step. If you don't know anything about photography and filming and you own an expensive camera, a photographer or a cinematographer with a phone can outmatch you. It's all in the skill. Of course, I'm not saying you don't need a decent camera—you can graduate to a DSLR camera in the future if you want to. But you can start with just your smartphone, so let's start with the cheapest alternative, which is your phone plus the basic skills you need.

So, for your phone, I recommend getting a camera app that can provide you with full control over your phone's camera settings. The most popular app for this would be the "FilMic pro," which is available in iOS and Android. There are a lot of camera apps available out there, so you can try and see which one works best for you first. But if your phone's native camera app gives you the option to manually adjust the settings, then go right ahead.

First up, adjust the white balance. Make sure that it's not too cool and not too warm. It actually depends more on your vibe and the temperature of your videos. Just don't overdo it—something too blue will make you look like you're in a freezer, or you're an alien or something.

Next, set the bit rate to the highest setting you possibly can. You'd want to film in 1080p because even though YouTube supports 4K videos, the huge file size will take longer to edit, render, and upload. So unless you have a really strong desktop computer and a super-fast internet connection, filming in 1080p is recommended. Your viewers are more inclined to notice the bad audio quality of your video than the difference if you shot it in 4k or 1080p.

And then there's this basic rule for filmmaking, which is the 180° shutter rule. This means that your shutter speed should be double your frame rate or FPS. The ideal frame rate would be 24 or 25 FPS with your shutter speed at 1/50th. This captures the scene the same way the human eye perceives them. In short, this gives you the "realistic" motion blur that you see in movies, or the "cinematic blur" as some might say. Of course, you can adjust the settings as you see fit, and break the rules, per se. Just remember that the faster the shutter speed (1/60th above), the darker your video gets, and it also gives you less motion blur as it lets in less light. However, it goes the opposite way if you slow down your shutter speed (1/30th below), producing a brighter scene and more blur. The 180° rule applies for DSLR cameras, too, so keep this rule in mind for future reference.

You would also need a tripod and a phone clamp. You can actually attach smartphones to any tripod if you have a phone mount or an adapter. This way, you can just keep using the same tripod when you decide to upgrade to a DSLR. But if you can manage to get steady shots by propping your phone up with things you find lying around in the house, then that's great too!

As for the audio, check your phone's built-in microphone quality first. Most built-in microphones will work fine if you're just starting out. The quality is not bad, but if the one on your phone is really terrible (so much so that it makes you sound like you're in a can, for example), you might want to upgrade.

People would prefer to watch low-res videos with good audio than sit through one with horrible audio, even if you shot it in 4k. Thankfully, there's a lot of good and cheap wireless microphones and lavalier (lav or clip-on) mics you can get online. "Rode Wireless Go" would be the most popular one and also the most expensive too. On the other end of the spectrum would be "Boya BY-M1". It's cheap but still delivers amazing quality. A special shout-out goes to "Joby Wavo," which is made for smartphone vlogging. For those planning to do voice-overs, just a good-quality headset can already work wonders for your content.

Also, don't forget to shoot with your rear camera—it has better specs than your front cam. If you're worried about not seeing your shots while recording, you can just mirror your phone screen to your laptop or your computer while shooting. If you don't have that option, use the front cam to find the perfect spot to frame your shot first, test shoot, then flip it to use the rear cam when you're finally shooting.

For framing the shot, you'd want to use natural light—it's the best light source, it's free, it's strong, and has this hue that makes your skin look fresh! So, figure out which part of your house, office, or room has light coming in at which time of the day, then set up in front of the window. Sitting facing the window can mirror the effect of a ring light or a soft box, so that's great for beauty vloggers while sitting with the window to your side can let you have this dramatic split lighting effect. And if you really want to invest in video equipment, I suggest starting off with your lighting equipment. This way, you can shoot at any time of the day or night, no matter what the weather is outside. You can start with just one at first, depending on what video you'll want to be shooting.

Here's a quick rundown on some lights that you can consider:

The ring light, as I mentioned before, is for beauty vloggers. It eliminates almost all shadows on the subject and has this characteristic ring or halo catchlight for your eyes.

Softboxes, on the other hand, mimic natural light and have wider coverage. This particular light is preferred for indoor vlogs, cooking shows, and just all-around videos. Get this one first if you're not a beauty vlogger.

Umbrella light produces more directional and controlled

light coverage. It's portable too and cheaper, but a lot harder to manage. It has mainly two types: the shoot through, which shoots the light through the fabric of the umbrella hence casting a softer light on the subject, and the reflective, which makes the light bounce from the reflective fabric of the umbrella onto the subject. This particular light is preferably used for indoor vlogs.

And lastly, let's talk about the different cameras you can consider when you want to upgrade from your mobile phone. A lot of YouTubers eventually graduate to DSLR cameras like the "Panasonic GH5" and the "Sony ZV-1", but some people prefer action cameras like the "DJI Osmo Pocket" and "GoPro Hero 8 Black" for outdoor shots. So here are a few things you need to consider when looking for cameras:

The articulating screen, as this allows you to see the screen when you're trying to film yourself

A good autofocus (get one with face or eye tracking, especially if you tend to move around a lot)

Built-in stabilization to minimize that shaky, dizzying footage that makes you look like you're filming the sequel for The Blair Witch Project (or get a gimbal)

Also, check for the mic inputs and hot shoe for mounting microphones and live streaming options.

The Best Editing Software to Choose From (Depending on Your Budget)

It can be overwhelming when you're looking for the best video editing software to personally use, especially when you're a beginner in all this. There are many options out there with varying price ranges. So, first, pick something that fits your budget. Second, it should be user-friendly to you. There will be a steep learning curve with all these software, and some will come more easily to you, so look for something that makes sense to you. The third thing to look for is the features and what it can offer—you would want software that can let you do everything you want to do easily with the features it has on hand.

The industry standard for video editing would be the Adobe Premier Pro (Windows and Mac), which can be used in conjunction with Adobe After Effects (Windows and Mac) or any of the Adobe Suite programs. Adobe Premier is more for editing, while Adobe After Effects lets you create animations and effects. You can link the compositions you made in After

Effects in the video you're editing in Premier, too—no problem!

Premier is easy enough to use, but it comes with a hefty price tag. Another software that professional video editors use is Final Cut Pro (Mac only). Since Final Cut is made by Apple, it will make perfect sense for long-time Apple users and can be linked with your Mac's Photos and iTunes. Both software can let you try them out for a number of days, so try your hand at editing videos on both of them to know which suits you more. These two come highly recommended, and it will make sense if you try learning them if you want to do YouTube full-time, as you will probably graduate to either of these two in the end, anyway.

There's also Adobe Premier Elements (Windows and Mac), which is the more affordable cousin of Premier Pro. It isn't as complicated as Premier Pro but still comes with a lot of the features you'll be looking for. Next is Adobe Premiere Rush, the other smaller Adobe cousin, made specifically for your phone. It's a lot simpler than both but still comes with some of the best features professionals love in Pro. It's IOS and Android compatible, so you can edit your videos on the go.

Meanwhile, a crowd favorite for beginners and enthusiasts,

on the other hand, would be Filmora9 (Windows and Mac). It's intuitive, so this will be easier for beginners and also has a lot of effects to choose from. There's a free version, but your videos will have Filmora's watermark. There are a few options, though, like the one-year plan, the lifetime plan, and the unlimited plan.

The Corel VideoStudio Ultimate (Windows only) is a great tool for beginners too. And since it belongs to the Corel suite family, it's well-designed and intuitive to boot. For its affordable price range, it has pretty good features.

Pinnacle Studio (Windows only) is another good choice for beginners—it's also cheaper than any of the software mentioned above. It's not as comprehensive as the others, but it will do if you're just starting out. However, if you want a browser editing option, there's always the "Vimeo Create" (IOS, Android, and Browser) specifically made for creating professional-looking social media videos. This is especially great for absolute beginners as it comes with free video templates, stock videos, and even music clips. Sadly, it comes with membership as it's used in conjunction with the other Vimeo apps. It has a free 30-day trial, though.

But as I said, there's still a handful of editing software out there. If you really can't get the hang of the paid ones or just can't deal with the price tag, for now, I'll discuss the free ones below. These might not come with the range of features the paid ones have, but most of them are powerful enough to do their job well. If you can work your way around the restrictions creatively, you can still come out with a great video for your channel.

I'm going to start with the basics. Usually, these are the ones people go for when they are absolute beginners as they are, again, free. Some of them even come pre-packaged in your OS (no download necessary!).

So, YouTube actually has its own web-based editing software

that's very easy to use, which you can just simply access using your browser. The built-in video editor in your YouTube Creator Studio offers you the most basic functions you need when editing videos. It allows you to "Add an End screen" (it's that screen that prompts your viewers to watch a related playlist and to subscribe to your channel) and edit already published videos without losing the video URL and ID. But you need to upload a video first and keep it as unlisted or private before you can start with your editing process.

Apple iMovie (Mac only) comes preloaded in your Mac. For free software, iMovie packs quite a punch—you'll have no problem churning out professional-looking videos by just using just this software. It can even help you add titles, effects, and transitions!

And then, of course, there's the Windows equivalent—the Windows Photo App. This one comes free for Windows 10 users, so you can try to update to Windows 10 first. The software allows you to do basic video editing and also has a feature that allows you to export directly to YouTube. If you can't update to Windows 10, there's another pretty good Windows editing software that everyone knows about—the Windows Movie Maker. Sadly, Microsoft doesn't support this app anymore, so you need to download this from third party sites. It comes with a handful of effects and features that, again, lets you do basic editing.

For editing videos on the go, there's Videorama (iOS only) and Videoshop (Android and iOS). Both apps are very easy to use and have a handful of fun filters and effects in their arsenal. They also allow you to do voice overs easily. There's also KineMaster (Android and iOS), another phone-based editing app. This app is powerful enough even for professionals on the go but is still easy enough for beginners to use. With its positive reviews from critics, this is arguably the best phone editing app out there.

Still, there will probably come a time when you find yourself restricted with the features the above software can offer and want to do more with your videos, so here's a list for those looking for something more advanced but still easy on the budget:

Shotcut (Windows, Linux, Mac) is a step up from the basic editing software I've mentioned above. If you have outgrown the Windows photo app or feel restricted with the YouTube Creator Studio but are scared to dabble with the heavy hitters in this list, then this is perfect for you. With its huge array of easy-to-apply filters and wonderful special effects, it's also very easy to use with its customizable interface. Plus, it has a good number of file formats to boot for when you're ready to export.

Lightworks (Windows, Linus, and Mac) delivers cinematic grade videos that won't cost a dime. It's harder to get the hang of, but it's worth learning as some major Hollywood productions have used the software. The free version doesn't have much difference in terms of features from the paid one, except that you can only export your videos at 720p, which is totally fine; 720p is still HD. Also, there's a lot of tutorials online, so don't worry about the learning curve.

DaVinci Resolve (Windows, Mac, and Linux), like Lightworks, has been used in some big-budget productions as well. Also, like Lightworks, it has a paid version, but their free version gives you access to just as many features. This software has some great audio and color correction capabilities under its belt and allows for multi-user collaboration (this could help a lot with big projects or collabs).

Hitfilm (Windows and Mac) lets you directly upload to YouTube and gives you professional-grade results with 3D effects without breaking the bank. The free version has the basics and more of what you need when editing your videos, but if you find it lacking, it offers paid add-on features so you can curate the software for your own use within your budget. The downside is that it needs a powerful laptop or computer to make it run smoothly.

And finally, with all these editing software to choose from, you need to remember a few pointers:

Use the widescreen format (16:9 ratio) when editing to avoid getting your video cropped or squeezed to fit. Don't add borders or black bars. YouTube will add it automatically when they're needed.

The ideal video dimension is again 1080p or 1920 x 1080, but you can drop down to 720p. This will still let your viewers watch your videos in HD.

Keep your file size to a maximum of 128GB.

Though a few of the options I've given you let you export directly to YouTube, some don't. Here are the video formats YouTube accepts at the moment: .mp4, .avi, .wmv, .mpeg, .mpegps, .mov, .flv, 3GPP and . webM.

How to Actually Upload a Video

And so it begins: you're finally ready for your first upload. The instructions seem never-ending, don't they? Don't fret. It may all look confusing at first, but when you finally get the hang of it, it'll all pay off in the end.

So let's say you have your video file on hand, all ready to be launched. You took pains and made sure it's in the right format, size, and ratio.

Sign in to your YouTube account and go to YouTube Creator Studio. On the upper right-hand corner of your screen, right beside your profile or channel icon, you'll see the Create button.

Clicking this will give you a drop-down menu for uploading your video and live streaming (in here, live streaming is "Go Live"). You can also access these functions by clicking the "Upload" and "Go Live" icons below the "Create" button.

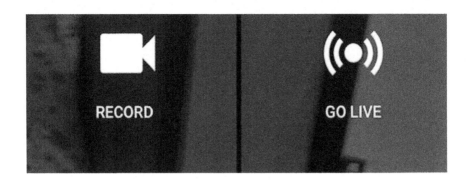

On the Upload page, you can drag-and-drop your selected file, and you will be promptly brought to a page where you can enter the details about your video. Under Details, you can type in the video title, descriptions, and upload your well-crafted video thumbnail and add your video to an existing playlist. You can also create a new playlist on the spot. This page also lets you specify who your audience will be. Is this made for kids? Is there an age restriction? Tags and closed captions or subtitles can also be added from this page.

The Video Elements tab lets you add an "End Card" and various other "Cards". Note: you can't add an "End Card" or "Cards" to videos you marked as made for kids. Adding cards to your video allows you to promote your other videos, other users, or your channel. At the same time, you can also add a Subscribe button and your channel icon here. This could be your CTA or "Call-To-Action" button.

Lastly, under the Visibility tab, you can choose who can see and when you want to publish your video. The "Schedule" option lets you specify the exact date and time you'd like your video to be made public. This option is a great tool for you to consistently keep up with the set schedule of your new video releases. Think of this as the time slot for a series that you are looking forward to (e.g., "new episodes every Friday night!" or something of the like). This can create hype and help make your viewers look forward to your new releases.

Made a mistake and clicked "Done" too fast? Don't worry—from your YouTube Creator Studio, you can access your video by clicking the video icon on the toolbar to your left. Edit different aspects of your videos easily by clicking the detail or pen icon when you hover over the video thumbnail. From here, you can even edit the whole video by using the in-house or in-browser video editor.

How to Grow Your Channel and Actually Make Money

Already have your channel all prepped and ready to go? Good! The only problem is that your first video is up, but you don't have subscribers or views just yet (okay; maybe a handful from your supportive friends or your doting grandma who'll announce to all her friends in her book club that you're a star now). But still, how do you get from zero views and zero subscribers to a hundred to thousands of subscribers?

Here's the cold, harsh truth—it's not going to be easy. It will take time before your channel can pick up speed and start racking up those views. No YouTuber will tell you that they started out with one video that went viral from the start. Some unicorns might have been able to do the impossible, but one thing's for certain—that just means that they already had a solid following from the start, even before they started their YouTube account.

But now that you've found your niche and you followed the correct branding strategies, you know that you have amazing content. So how do you come up in the YouTube search engine or in the suggested videos for all the viewers out there?

A lot of articles mention YouTube SEO optimization or "Search Engine Optimization." This basically means letting the algorithm know what your video is about by inserting relevant keywords in your content metadata, thus improving the chances of your videos coming up in the search engine when people type in queries.

Your metadata pertains to your content's title, tags, description, and video. And then there's Suggested Video Optimization, where you optimize your metadata to help boost the chances of your video being in the Suggested Videos when viewers are watching popular content.

YouTube Algorithm

I could just give you a list of the tools and things you'll need to do, but I feel like you need an understanding of how the algorithm works, so you know the "Why" of what you're doing. Now, the algorithm has changed a bit over the years, so what I'm discussing now might be outdated in the coming years, but YouTube releases updates for its creators regularly on its own channels called "Creator Insider" and "YouTube Creators." In "YouTube Creators," they also release tutorials on different topics from the algorithm to copyright and monetization. It would be a good idea to subscribe to these two channels for your own sake. They also have a website called "YouTube Creator Academy" that tackles all the different kinds of topics you'll need.

Now, on to the algorithm.

The algorithm YouTube put in place has two main goals, namely, finding the right video for the right viewer and to make them keep watching more videos for longer periods of time, thus seeing more ads.

The basics of this are that YouTube looks into a lot of places to know more about your video. They look at your video title, description, thumbnails, tags, and even listen to your audio to know what your video is all about. Using the data gathered about your video and its performance, the algorithm then searches for the right viewer to match it with. To know of the video's performance, the algorithm looks at the following:

How many clicks the video gets

The video's watch time, like how long your viewers watch the video for, whether they stick to the end or click out after a few seconds

They also look in on how many likes and comments the video gets

How new the video is

To know whether the viewer will like a certain video or not is all about personalization. This depends on the viewers' watch history, which refers to:

How long they spent watching the topic

What channels and topics have they subscribed to and watched

What video they liked and commented on

There are a few places where the algorithm pushes your videos to potential viewers. These are the Home Page or sometimes what they call Browse, the Suggested Videos, and the YouTube search. These three are the main sources of where your new viewers will be coming from. It might not be the same for everyone—for instance, for cooking videos, the bulk of their new viewers will come from the searches. The other places where your videos can be discovered are in the trending tabs, the subscription tabs, and the notifications.

🏠 **Home**

🔥 Trending

📑 Subscriptions

▶️ Library

🕐 History

▶️ Your videos

🕐 Watch later

There's not much you can do to make your video appear in

the Trending tab—this one depends more on how your video is faring, nor in the subscriptions and notifications if the viewers aren't subscribed to your channel. So let's talk more about how the algorithm works in Home, Suggested Videos, and Search.

The YouTube homepage is the site's main landing page. Keep in mind that videos that appear here are not the same for every person. This is where people discover new videos to watch when they just open up the website casually and don't have a specific thing in mind to see. The videos that appear here range from new videos to videos that are watched by similar viewers and some of the viewer's subscriptions. What makes new videos appear in a viewer's YouTube home page is based on two things: how well the video has performed and personalization.

You can find the Suggested Videos on the right side of the screen when you're watching a video or below the video on your mobile devices. Note the roster of videos here is also different for everyone. The videos that appear here come from what the viewer is currently watching, videos on related topics, and the viewer's watch history. How the new videos appear here, however, are based on the viewer's watch history and personalization.

On YouTube search, the algorithm matches the video's metadata to whatever the viewer has typed in the query. Again, this is the video's title, description, tags, and even the closed caption. It also looks into the video's watch time and how well the video has matched to past queries. And again, due to the algorithm's personalization, what appears in one person's search query might differ from another person's results.

Keywords and Metadata

Now that you have a better understanding of how the algorithm works, you can use it to help your videos appear in the three main stages on YouTube where your videos can be discovered. This is where the keywords come in. I touched on keywords briefly when talking about what your channel will be about—now, let's talk about them more in detail. Let's start with keywords and metadata.

There's a number of tools that can help you with your keyword search to help you figure out what people are searching for. You do this to know what words to use in your title, descriptions, tags, and thumbnails. "Can't I just write whatever I want to title my video?" You can, but it's better if you put in the right keywords, so your video comes up in their search or in the suggested videos.

You should also use keywords in your video description. A lot of YouTubers make the mistake of just writing their social media accounts and website links in the description box. You still can, but it's better if you insert them later at the bottom. Because YouTube's algorithm also uses your video's description box to know more about your content, front load your description with a short paragraph about your video. Try to mention your top keywords in the first three sentences, keeping the most relevant information on top so people can see it without clicking "Read More."

Don't be lazy and just copy your title—YouTube doesn't like that. Change the phrases up, so they still mean the same but are written differently. For example, if your title is "Quick and Easy Overnight Oats Recipe/Easy Hack for Breakfast," in the description box, you can type, "This is my healthy and delicious overnight oats recipe that is perfect for those lazy mornings. It's a fast and simple breakfast hack that's also perfect for those rushed mornings!"

Also, don't trick your viewers with a top keyword or a clickbait title and deliver something entirely different in your video. Using the example above, your viewers click your video expecting an overnight oats recipe. If all they see is you blabbering on and on about arranging flowers in your kitchen with just the last three minutes showing your overnight oats recipe, it's not going to bode well for you or your channel.

Another good practice for your description box is to include all the relevant information that you think your viewers will appreciate. When you watch videos, and you click on the description box, don't you sometimes wish that there was more information? Let's say you are a musician, and you just released a new song, and you performed it live and recorded it. In the description, you can type in a brief description of your new song. After the line break, type in your song lyrics and the software and instruments you used in your recorded performance. You can also include your social media accounts and website for faster access.

If you're doing a report about an obscure piece of history in the Philippines, it's best practice to credit your sources too and add links to related articles that helped you during your research. If you did a tutorial about growing different kinds of produce at home, add timestamps to all the different segments of your videos. It will not hurt to advertise your products in the description box too! You got their attention, and they are watching your videos, so add CTAs or Call to Action buttons to Like, to Buy your products, or to Subscribe or watch your other playlists.

But the keywords don't just reside in your title and description box. Remember when I said that YouTube listens to your videos? The algorithm also relies on closed captioning to understand what your video is about, so it's best practice to drop those keywords in when you're speaking in the video or in the subtitles. It also helps when you add your subtitles yourself. Not only will it broaden your range of viewers—making your videos go international if you submit it in another language—but it lessens the risk of YouTube's auto-translate bot mishearing what you said and placing you in an entirely different category. You also type in those well-researched keywords in your channel's about page, in your hashtags, and tags.

Optimization and Using the Algorithm to Help Boost Your Channel

There are two ways on how to optimize your content for YouTube. SEO is optimizing your videos to appear in YouTube queries by using trending and optimized keywords in your video's metadata. Steer clear of general keywords that cover large and popular topics, like "Outfit Ideas" or "Bedroom DIY." Try to be more specific, and find related keywords. You can use tools like TubeBuddy and ViDIQ to help you find a stronger keyword. So instead of using "Bedroom DIY," you can instead consider "Bedroom DIY Decorating Ideas." It will pull your video out of those millions of "Bedroom DIY" videos so it won't drown in the sea of content.

There's another way: search for your competitors, popular or not, on YouTube, and see what they're typing. Copy a few of their predominant keywords and use them on yours. This is what others call suggested video optimization. The algorithm can then recommend your video to people with similar viewing preferences when they are watching your competitor's video.

Let's say your video is about the funny, derpy antics your cat Bernie does on an everyday basis, and you want to make this into a vlog series. You want to title the videos "Bernie's Everyday Adventures," but then with nearly no subscribers and views, who will know who Bernie is? No one out there will search for Bernie and expect a funny cat video. So you can rename this to "My Funny and Stupid Cat/Bernie's

Adventure/Funny Cat Vlog 1" You use the word "stupid" instead of "derpy" because Google Trends show there's a higher number of people using the search word "stupid cat" than "derpy cat." Also, looking at YouTube searches, the view counts for "stupid cat" is higher than the latter.

It really depends on your content when choosing the kind of optimization you want to use. Like for recipes and cooking videos, a large portion of the traffic for these comes from searches as people are specific when looking for recipes on YouTube. For vlogs, on the other hand, most will come from suggested videos. Look at your YouTube analytics to figure out where the main source of your traffic comes from. If you find out that most of them come from Suggested Videos and Browse, then optimize your keywords for that and vice versa.

Next, let's figure out how to use your knowledge about the algorithm to help you boost your channel's stats. YouTube's algorithm is actually there to help you. They want to push your video to the right viewers to make them keep watching videos. And since knowing that YouTube depends on your videos' metadata and performance, you can use this to craft better videos and practices.

Let's talk about a few tricks on how to boost your video's

performance, which depends on how well the viewers like your video.

Always Start With Good, Compelling Content

Craft a good video thumbnail. It's good practice to mock up your thumbnail to see how it looks in different sizes, like on the homepage, in Suggested Videos, and how it looks on mobile. Putting too many words might help people who see it on the homepage understand what it's about better, but then everything will be too crowded when you see the same thumbnail in the Suggested Videos section. The thumbnail is smaller over there, so people might just scroll past it. The same is true with your video descriptions, About, and Title— see whether or not anything gets cut off, and make the necessary adjustments.

Upload regularly. The algorithm will regularly push new videos to the centerstage for it to gain traction, so uploading consistently can help you have more videos out there to push out.

Make sure your thumbnails, title, description, and videos match. Viewers will stop watching a video if they click on it and find out that it's not what they're looking for.

Make a series or a playlist. This will help your videos show up in the suggested videos.

Add CTA to your videos by adding cards. Link to your channel and other your videos that might be connected to the video on hand.

Also, don't be embarrassed to ask your viewers to Like, Subscribe, Comment, and even "Hit the notification bell to stay updated on new videos."

Engage with your viewers. The algorithm also looks at your viewer engagement, so Liking a few of the comments can make your viewers happy and may lead to more Likes and more comments. Craft your videos in a way that encourages your viewers to engage more.

Keep your videos consistent. Stay on track.

Don't make your video's intro too long. Be concise and jump in on the topic as soon as possible. You don't want them to leave your video in the middle of your long and winding intro, as this will hurt your video's watch time or performance. Keep them watching. It doesn't matter if your video is long or short as long as it holds your viewers' interest, and they watch through the end.

Pay attention to seasonal and trending topics. I'm not saying you should copy others; put your own twist in it, and think of what you can bring to the table.

Listen to your viewer's feedback. Use YouTube Analytics to understand more about your viewers and, at the same time, be adaptable. Let's say you started your channel with women in their early thirties in the US as your target audience in mind. After posting a few of your videos, you see that the bulk of your views come from Japan and South Korea and are popular among college students. You can adapt to your new market, then study why they like your video and the trends there.

If something works, stick to it. For example, you've been making DIY videos for a while now, but suddenly your videos about modern tapestry weaving spiked up in views. Maybe you should start concentrating on those videos or make a series. Sometimes, it just takes one upsurge, and you can easily cling to it and make it your own official cash cow.

If you watch YouTube's "Creator Insider," their tagline is "Keep it real." I feel like this resonates a lot with how you would work on your channel. Using your knowledge about the algorithm properly can surely put your videos out there, but then YouTube also looks at your video's performance. Your thumbnails and perfectly keyworded metadata will mean nothing if people click your videos and leave after a few seconds, as this will impact your video's performance negatively. Your clicks and views might increase, but after the algorithm sees that your video's watch time is non-existent, it will stop pushing your videos out there. So no click-bait titles! It's best to be honest and craft wonderful, amazing, and engaging content and, at the same time, use your added YouTube SEO and algorithm knowledge to give your videos a proper push.

Tools to Help You

There's a number of tools that can come in handy when you start researching your keywords, competitors, and data. Some call them YouTube marketing tools; some call them YouTube analytics tools. A few of them have a paid premium membership, and some of them are free, but let's delve into what YouTube already has: YouTube Analytics.

As I said, YouTube wants to help you, the content creators, come up with amazing content that people can't stop watching. And to know more about what kind of quality content your viewers like to watch, YouTube has its own analytics to help you streamline your content. By logging in to your account and accessing the YouTube Creator Studio, you can immediately see basic data about your most recent video and your channel's overall analytics in the dashboard. This includes important info like the number of subscribers you have, your views, and the watch time in the last 28 days as well as the top videos of your channel in the last 48 hours.

To go even more in-depth, you can go to your analytics page by clicking the analytics chart icon from the toolbar on your left. YouTube analytics gives you an in-depth look at how your channel is faring. You can look at your numbers in correlation to specific videos, video groups, and playlists, or just the whole channel in general. What's great about this is that it also shows you your viewer's demographics, i.e., the age range, gender, and the countries where they live in so you can adjust how you'd want to pivot your channel.

In the "Reach" tab, you can also see where most of your traffic is coming from and your video's click through rate or CTR. This is shown in the impressions card or what they call the "Funnel." The "Funnel" will show you how many people have seen your thumbnails and the percentage and numbers of how many have actually clicked at your video. It also shows you how many viewers watched it and the average watch time of that certain video. By looking at the CTR, you can see how effective your video thumbnails and titles are.

This is mostly your thumbnail's doing, so if your CTR is especially low, you can consider changing your thumbnail to something more attractive or eye-catching.

YouTube counts thirty seconds of watch time as one view. It will still count as one view if a viewer skips through different parts of your video but still accumulates thirty seconds of watch time. Now, divide your watch time by your number of views, and you get your average view duration. If your videos have a high average view duration, this means you are keeping viewers on the website, and the algorithm will start pushing it out to more viewers, automatically increasing your video's chances at appearing in the Suggested Videos and Home.

Channels with high retention rates always rank higher, so if viewers just watch the first few seconds of your video and decide to stop before hitting the thirty-second mark, your video's introduction may be far too long, and you're not getting into the topic fast enough. This means that you need to start thinking of ways to keep your viewers locked to your content. Luckily, you can also see audience retention rates easily so you can see which exact parts are interesting for your viewers and which parts make them lose interest just as quickly.

And if you use the advanced mode on the upper right hand of the analytics page, it will show you an even more detailed analysis of your channel. You can even see what devices your viewers are primarily watching your videos from. Needless to say, pay attention to your channel's YouTube analytics. Explore it and use the data you have there to improve your channel.

Google Keywords Planner or Keywords Everywhere

Keywords Everywhere was a free tool until recently. It's a Google Chrome and Firefox extension that you can install in your browser to see the monthly search volume, the cost per click, and the competition data for every keyword that you type in Google and YouTube. It's a powerful tool that can let you know instantly how many people have searched the keyword in the past month. It also lets you know a lot at a glance by just typing a query on YouTube.

It has a pricing plan now, but you can still install it for free and see the trend data of keywords that you type in. To see the volume, you'd need to add credits, so if you can't spare a dollar or two, there's a free alternative—Google actually has a Keyword Planner inside Google Ads. Google Ads is free; you just need to create a new account and sign in. It will ask for billing info, but it can't charge you anything until you have a campaign registered, and a customer actually clicks on your ad or your website.

Go to "Tools and Settings" on the menu bar on top. Under "Planning," go to "Keyword Planner," and from there, you can compare multiple keywords based on multiple locations and see the average monthly searches.

TubeBuddy and VidIQ

Both tools are designed to help you boost your YouTube SEO. They are also extensions for your Chrome and Firefox browsers and are YouTube-certified. For both of them, most of their features about your channel's analytics in their free plans are already on YouTube Analytics. Where they both shine, however, is in helping you figure out the proper keywords to use and analyzing your competitor data. When you type in possible keywords in the search bar, you'll be given the keyword statistics and info, as well as a list of other related or suggested keywords that you can use to improve your score. Of course, you get more out of them with their paid plans.

You can download and use both of them at the same time just to test them out and see which one suits you best. It makes for a cluttered dashboard, so I suggest turning one of the extensions off when you're using the other and vice versa.

A Brief Discussion On YouTube's Guidelines for Monetizing Content

And now on to the part you've been waiting for: monetizing your content. Let's talk about how to make money on YouTube, but first, you need to qualify and apply for YPP or the YouTube Partner Program.

To qualify, you need to have at least four thousand public watch hours during the last twelve months, have reached one thousand subscribers, and have a good standing with YouTube—that means no violations or breaking YouTube community guidelines from the time you started. To know if you are qualified for YPP, you can go to your YouTube Studio dashboard and click the monetization icon, which is that little dollar icon on the toolbar to your left. Scroll to the bottom of the page, and you'll see a counter telling you how many subscribers and public watch hours you have left before you hit the threshold. Once you're eligible to apply, YouTube will ask you to sign the Program terms, and you need to sign up for a Google AdSense account.

After you apply, a member of the YouTube staff will review your application and will normally get back to you in a month. If your application is approved, all you have to do is stay active by uploading videos. There's also no threshold to meet every year after you get approved. But if you do fall below the one thousand subscriber threshold AND your channel is inactive for months, then YouTube might remove you from the program.

There are times when an application will be rejected. This will likely be because the application didn't meet the YPP and YouTube community guidelines. Still, you can apply again after 30 days, but in the meantime, review the guidelines and edit or remove the videos that break them.

Next, let me give you a brief intro on how YouTube ads work. There are three players when it comes to monetizing your videos on YouTube: the creator, the advertisers, and the viewers. Creators create content that attracts a certain demographic. The advertisers can then target that specific demographic your videos cater to and pay YouTube and you for their ads watched, displayed, or clicked. When you are a member of the YPP or YouTube Partner Program, you can choose to place ads in your videos to monetize your content. There are different types of ads that you can choose to apply to your content. These are:

Skippable and non-skippable video ads - these ads appear before your video plays. For skippable ads, your viewers can choose to skip the ad after 5 seconds. Note that YouTube doesn't count a skipped ad as a view; as such, the advertiser doesn't have to pay, and you also don't get paid.

Display non-video ads (these appear on the right or below of the video, above the suggested videos)

Mid-roll ads are ads that appear in the middle of long-form videos. YouTube just changed the limit of long-form videos by the way—now, you can use mid-roll ads on videos that are eight minutes or longer. Mid-roll ads work like those mid-show commercials. You can choose to manually insert these ads where you want them to be in your video by using the YouTube video editor, or you can just let YouTube automatically add these anywhere in your video.

Overlay ads. These ads appear semi-transparent on

the lower 20% of your video and will stay there while your video is playing.

Bumper ads are non-skippable ads played before your video starts and are up to 6 seconds long. You can turn this and a skippable video ad on, and they'll play one after the other before your video starts.

And then you have sponsored ads. These appear for a few seconds as cards in your video and may display content that's related to your video.

On the surface, a YouTuber gets paid every time a viewer watches an ad or clicks it. But a YouTuber's income is also affected by how much an advertiser is paying to reach certain demographics. Here are a few factors that can affect your revenue:

Your video's viewers will affect the amount of revenue that you'll receive. Advertisers look for a certain demographic to target for their brand. If your videos serve a popular demographic with advertisers looking to advertise on YouTube, it will definitely affect your revenue.

The length of your video - if your video is longer, you can cram in more ads, which leads to more revenue

The quality and topic of your content - let's say you have a longer video, and you cram in as many ads as you can, without overdoing it, but then your topic isn't that popular, or what you're serving isn't quality content. Sadly, only a few viewers will see your ad.

Different keywords attract different advertisers.

There are certain types of people who are more apt to use ad blockers. So if your viewers tend to install ad blockers, you won't see a single cent coming from ads.

The quality of ads that come up in your videos also affects your views. If the advertiser or brand targeting your viewers come up with more engaging and creative ads, there are more chances that your viewers won't skip the ad and might even click it. This means a larger payout for you too.

YouTube also introduced a new monetization metric in YouTube Analytics: RPM or revenue per mille. This shows how much a creator is earning per one thousand views.

Before RPM, YouTube used CPM (cost per mille), which is an advertiser-based metric. This shows the cost per one thousand views.

RPM, on the other hand, is a creator-based metric. This shows you how much you're earning compared to CPM, which just shows you how much the advertiser is paying. It is calculated as "total revenue" divided by the "total views" multiplied by one thousand. Total revenue includes all revenues the creator earns, from ads, channel membership, YouTube premium, Super Chat, and Super Stickers, then subtracted with YouTube's revenue share. Total views mean all views from public, private, and unlisted videos plus the views from live streams, even from unarchived ones.

So, now that that's out of the way let's talk about the different ways you can earn money on YouTube now that you're on YPP. These are by advertising revenues, YouTube Premium Revenue, channel memberships, merchandise shelves, super chats, and super stickers. However, there are eligibility requirements you must meet in order to be able to turn on these monetization features.

For ad revenues from views, you must be at least 18 years of age; if you're younger, have a legal guardian older than 18 to handle your payments using Google AdSense.

For channel memberships, again, you must be at least 18 years old, and your channel should have reached 30,000 subscribers.

To be eligible for the merchandise shelf, you should be 18 years old and have 10,000 subscribers.

With Super Chat and Super Stickers, you must be 18 years old and above and live in a place where Super Chat is available

For YouTube Premium revenue, you just need to create content that's viewed by a YouTube Premium subscriber.

You can also earn money by crowdfunding, creating sponsored content, licensing your content to media outlets (for when your content goes viral), and joining or organizing events. I'll briefly introduce you to all of these, but let's start first with Ad revenue.

Earning money from ads is the first thing you would want to do after you've become a member of YPP. YouTube actually recommends turning on all types of ads for all your videos to increase your ad revenue. In order to allow ads to be displayed on your video, your content must be advertiser-friendly and not made for kids. Avoid controversial topics, too, as advertisers tend to steer clear of creators with controversial pasts and topics.

Channel memberships are where you let subscribers pay a monthly fee to become a member of your channel or community. This is where they can access member-exclusive perks like emojis, badges, etc. Inside, you can make membership levels with different price points. These levels add on top of each other, so members of the highest level also have access to the perks in the lower levels.

Here's a list of perks you can create inside: members only videos, community posts, live chats, and streams. You can also create custom channel badges and emojis. Think of this as a way to reward your most loyal and supportive subscribers without alienating the others that can't afford it. What do I mean? For example, some channels may offer an earlier release or a little behind-the-scenes footage of some videos to members. Here's an added tip: create a video explaining your channel membership and its perks to your viewers so they can understand why you're doing this.

In some countries, YouTube allows you to promote your merch on your video's end screen and on the merchandise shelf located below the description box. A lot of creators sell merch as another way to earn more money on the platform. Your merch must be unique to you and should be something that represents your channel that your subscribers would really like to buy. This could be anything from a badge proudly worn to proclaim that they are your subscribers or just a simple shirt with an inside joke printed on the front. To get an idea of what your viewers might like, just look into the comments section—and if you decide to create your own merch, remember to promote it in your videos.

Another way to earn big money on the side is when you create sponsored content for brands. This is great because you deal with the advertiser or brand directly, and YouTube won't take a revenue cut from it. If your channel is huge enough and you have targeted a popular demographic that the advertisers are looking for, brands would love to hear from you. They might even offer you deals to review, talk about, or use in your videos.

You might also want to sign up for marketing platforms for influencers. These help advertisers and marketing teams look for the perfect influencer that can promote their brand.

These are not limited to Instagram influencers, either, as some of them include YouTube personalities in their roster. Besides, videos pay higher because they're harder to make.

Remember to be careful about the brands that you partner with. It should be a brand that you're happy to promote, so it helps if you're actually using their products. Your subscribers would like to see you promote something that you really like or are using. It's also good if you can establish a reputation that you only promote something that you approve of. At the same time, always be transparent when it comes to promoting brands because these are essentially paid to advertise. Let your audiences know if you're paid to do the content for the brand by using YouTube's visible disclosure feature—it's that overlay on your video that says, "includes paid promotion."

And then there's what YouTube calls Super Chat and Super Stickers. These are essentially a feature that allows viewers to make their comments more visible during your live stream. Super Chat is a highlighted chat while Super Sticker is an animated sticker. Both get placed above the chat for a set amount of time in order to get ample time to get noticed. The larger the amount a viewer pays, the longer their Super Chats and Super Stickers stay on top. You just need to turn on the feature once, and live chats with Super Chats and Super Stickers will be available to all eligible premieres and live streams.

Don't be shy when promoting these features! Tell your audiences about it before you go on your live stream. Call out the names of people that used them and thank them personally. Your viewers will love it if you acknowledge them for their support.

Some YouTubers even tap into crowdfunding. Whether you're looking for ways to fund new equipment or you're trying to create channel-related content, crowdfunding can be an effective way to gather funds for your project.

For instance, say you're an illustrator or photographer who wants to make a book. You can use crowdfunding to pool money from your viewers. Patreon is great for recurring funding and is a common choice for YouTubers, while Kickstarter and GoFundMe are great for one big project like buying equipment, creating merch, or whatever you need that you think your viewers will pay for. And always remember to promote it on your channel.

When you create a video about dancing, twerking chihuahua

that just so happens to become an overnight sensation, news outlets may want to feature your video. When they want to use your content, they should and will pay. This is called licensing your content. It's important, then, to place your contact information for business inquiries in your About page in anticipation of the morning news channel that wants to share your hilarious clip of your sister dancing the Macarena under the influence of anesthesia.

But if you don't want to wait for that day when BBC comes calling, you can submit your videos to a video rights marketplace. This is where media outlets sometimes turn to in order to pad their news with something lighthearted. Check out Jukin media and Viral hog and submit your videos—you just never know!

And then there's joining or organizing events. When you already have a solid following, there will come a time in your YouTube career when you will have enough fans that follow you and would love to meet you in person. This is the perfect time to go join events like VidCon or other events for creators like yourself. You can also go to meetups organized by brands to visit their stores. This happens a lot for creators in fashion, beauty, and games.

There are a lot more ways to earn more by using the popularity you gain on YouTube. The cold, hard truth is that your YouTube career is not going to be around forever—people's interests change over time. There's always going to be a lot of fresh young faces and minds that can easily be the next big thing and overtake your track record completely.

So, don't stop school, don't quit your job, and don't sell all of your possessions until you're sure that the income your channel is generating is enough to support you. Once your YouTube channel grows in popularity, I suggest you invest your money and keep working like there's tomorrow. As long as you're still relevant, as long as your viewers haven't moved on to another creator, you need to use this popularity and success to build your connections.

Let's say you're a makeup guru. Consider collaborating with beauty brands in order to work with them and gain connections. In the future, you can even be a consultant—that's a more stable job with a more stable income. Use the popularity YouTube can give you to form business connections that would otherwise be harder to get with just a normal job. Always, always keep an eye out for more opportunities—the world is your oyster, after all!

How to Market Your YouTube Channel

There are many ways on how to let the world know about your channel or your new uploads. First is the most obvious thing, which is promoting it on your other social media accounts. If you already have a following on Instagram, Facebook, or TikTok, then jumping into the YouTube platform will be a breeze. Otherwise, use all possible platforms to promote.

Don't be shy, you're on YouTube now! So schedule your uploads and let people know what time and day you upload new videos. Post on your Instagram and Facebook accounts, and use appropriate hashtags and links to your videos. It can also help if you post little snippets or trailers about what your viewers can expect from your new upload. Tease them so they'll have to click on your link, and they'll watch your videos on YouTube.

Another angle to look at is to treat your channel as a, well, a channel! Create segments and sub-topics. For example, if you're a makeup guru, you can release videos every Friday about new looks. On Tuesday nights, you can have reviews about your favorite products. But at the end of your videos, don't forget to call out to your subscribers to Like and Subscribe and ask for what they want to see next—or better yet, give shoutouts to your most loyal subscribers so that they'll really feel special.

You can also partner with other upcoming YouTubers so you can promote each other's channels. Be open to collaborations! This is one thing that's great with YouTube—that sense of community that viewers love. Your viewers love it if their favorite YouTubers interact with each other, so contact some of those YouTubers that you follow, give them an amazing pitch, and convince them why they should collaborate with you. You can also ask your viewers about who they'd want to see you collaborate with—keeping them engaged with interactive questions will make them feel like they are relevant to your channel and that you really care about delivering quality content they will absolutely love.

Speaking of viewers, don't underestimate the power of "word of mouth." If you create really great content that your subscribers can't stop talking about, they will recommend you to their friends verbally, in social media, or even by Liking and sharing your content. Not only is this free publicity, but it also pulls your engagement ratings up, thereby making the YouTube algorithm push your video to other viewers who have similar interests. So show love to your viewers! They will be the foundations of your channel, always and forevermore.

Do giveaways and contests for your channel! This is a great way to earn new subscribers. Pick items that viewers can relate to your channel and would be valuable to them. Make it simple—it doesn't have to be a scavenger hunt. Just tell them to Like your videos, subscribe to your channel, and leave a comment! You can earn new subscribers, and your engagement ratings can easily rise up with something as simple as that.

When you also create your merch, try to incorporate your logo or channel into it. For instance, if you have shirts for sale with your logo on it, your subscribers will buy them and wear them around school or at the mall. That's essentially free advertising for you too!

You can also consider paid advertising in the form of YouTube ads. If you have the budget, this can be a great way to go—just try to make your ad as engaging and as click-worthy as you can so you won't be that annoying ad the viewers are dying to skip.

but don't forget your target audience.

Add CTAs to your videos. Ask your audiences to watch, Like, subscribe and click the notification bell.

Cross-promote your channel to different social media accounts.

Use keywords as a way to optimize your videos. Use them in your titles, descriptions, videos, and even on your About page.

Make playlists or a series to increase the chances of your videos appearing in the Suggested videos.

Post regularly. The algorithm likes to push out new content for viewers to watch.

Make great thumbnails. Studies show that viewers tend to click thumbnails with faces on them. You're a human being, after all, aren't you?

Engage with your audiences. This is a great way to build your subscriber base. Like and reply to their comments, ask them for their opinions, and listen to what your viewers are saying. Interaction is key!

Study your channel's analytics to find out how to improve your videos.

Don't forget to add cards and an end screen to promote your other content.

Keep at it and don't give up. It's hard work, but you'll get there. All YouTubers start with zero subscribers and views.

Make a channel trailer to introduce yourself.

Organize your videos into playlists. At the same time, create playlists of your more popular series. This will come up in the "Watch Next" portion when your viewers are watching your videos. Also, at the end of your video, tell your viewers about the series of videos that the current video they're watching now is part of.

Your video length doesn't matter. What matters is your video's watch time, so create content that's compelling and fun to watch to make sure that your viewers will watch until the end.

Study your demographics. Are they students? College students? Office workers? Housewives? Where do they live? Study their patterns and optimize your content for them. For example, high school students will have different concerns, wants, and needs compared to college students. Teenagers will likely be extremely concerned about reputations, identity, friendship, and belonging. They won't necessarily have everything figured out, but they know what's important to them, and your channel has to appeal to their value system and not just on the trends that are hip and popular among the youth.

Be wary of trends. If you play to current trends, that's just it—they're trends. These fads can come and go in an instant, and while there's nothing wrong with riding on a trend every so often, you can't rely on something like that as the core content of your channel.

YouTube is a social place. What makes it so popular is because the viewers feel closer to YouTubers through human interaction! Here's the thing: while algorithms, patterns, and all of those numbers are extremely important when it comes to SEO and all the financial stuff, don't forget that at the heart of it all is you—an actual human being. You're not a bot; isn't that exactly what you're sharing with your viewers through your channels? And because you're sharing the most human part of yourself in your content, the same is true for your viewers. They're not just numbers, Likes, and subscribers. They're not just usernames that comment on your videos and ring notifications. They're actual human beings like you, so don't forget that there's another human being just like you watching from the opposite end of the screen.

Always follow the YouTube Community and advertiser-friendly guidelines. You definitely wouldn't want to have all your hard work go to waste just because there's a teeny tiny loophole you missed in the guidelines. Getting banned after all that hard work is definitely not productive.

You also wouldn't want to anger your advertisers in any way—make sure that your partnerships will last a long, fruitful time so that you can both make the relationship as lucrative as possible. Make sure that the partnership is mutually beneficial, and you'll both ride off happily ever after into the sunset.

Follow copyright laws. Again, I can't stress this enough—your content has to be original, or you risk ruining your reputation and staining your name forever. Remember that it takes years of hard work to get original content out, and people take the time and all that effort to churn out something creative from the deepest depths of their creative wells. You can't just rip something off like that. While they say that imitation is the best form of flattery, nobody likes a copycat.

Don't feed the trolls! If you've ever heard of the joke that tells people never to venture into the Dreaded Comments Section, it's because there will always be random trolls who just want to watch the world burn.

While Internet trolls and keyboard warriors can be annoying, engaging them won't bring any kind of benefit to you or to your viewers at all, so hold your tongue (or fingers), leave them be, and just go on your merry way. If they're still persistently harassing you, you can always block them—life is too short to get mixed up with toxic people, right?

worthwhile is ever easy, and no, overnight YouTube sensations just don't exist. If you've ever stared longingly at the subscriber count of your YouTube idols with starry and glassy eyes wishing you could do the same, remember that it's not easy to make those numbers soar to skyrocketing heights.

These things take hard work. Behind all of those fancy and happy YouTubers you see on-screen are hours and hours spent poring over guidelines, rules, algorithms, SEOs, and technical stuff that the viewers don't really see when a video goes up. A lot of hard work goes into content before and after hitting that Upload button, so while I'm here to help you create your own YouTube channel and be a star yourself, I hope that knowing all of these challenges makes you develop a better appreciation and newfound respect for what other YouTubers do out there.

A lot of people will condescend you and look down on you when you start out with your YouTube career. Sadly, that's just the way human nature works when you reach for your dreams—people can be real Debbie Downers sometimes, especially when they've got a lot of crab mentality going on inside their heads. But you can always give those nay-sayers a run for their money once your channel is up and running.

That said, I would really love to know how things are going once you've got everything set up and ready to go. Who knows? I just might see you out there as the top live streamer raking in all that dough, or you might even come up with your own book someday. Until then, best of luck to you— you've got this!

Thank you for reading this book until the end. I hope it has helped you. Would you please consider leaving a like where you purchased this book online? Reviews help me reach a wider audience. Thanks in advance!